MODERN DAY POETRY

I MaryAnn Freeman a published song writer. Recorded on NCA GOLD ALBUM with Nashville country music. Songs includes Sad, I Have to Cry, You Better Watch, Coming Home for Christmas .Published poet received a certificate of recognition .From the United States of American. For copy right Modern Day Poetry. Listed in several books .Library of Congress and Who's Who in America. I received awards for my poems. Graduated from Barbizon School of Modeling and Nursing Assistant and Business School. I am a Inventor with a Design Patent from the United States Patent Office

POEMS

THE PRESENCE OF GOD

MY DECREE

SMILE

ROSES

ANGELS

THIS A DIVINE SET UP

KNOCKING AT YOUR KNOCK

HOME

THIS IS THE HOUSE GOD BLESS

MODERN DAY POETRY

THE WINTER I CAN NEVER FORGET

JERMAINE

SOLDIERS

IF I HAD MY OWN LAW

OFFICER DAN

CHILDREN

WHO SAID THAT A MAN IS NOT SUPPOSE TO CRY

TOO LITTLE

LOVE

MONEY

DARKNESS

MY KNIGHT

MAKING A DECISION

ROOM 1904

DOCTOR

MY UNIVERSE

MODERN DAY POETRY

LONG ISLAND

MODERN DAY POETRY

COUNTRY GIRL

MOTHER

BELIEVE

PEOPLE NEED TO LAUGH AGAIN

I HAD TO DIG DOWN DEEP

I LEARNED TO LOVE THY SELF

GIVING THANKS TO GOD

WRITER

COLOR

PAIN

PAID MY DUES

VICTORY

OPPORTUNITY

LIVING IN A WORLD OF MY OWN

.

MODERN DAY POETRY

DRUGS

THE CHILD THAT LIVES WITHIN MY WOMB

AWAKING

NO BODY LOVES ME

THE BLUE SKY

MODERN DAY POETRY

REACHING THE TOP

INSPIRE WRITER

OLD BILLY

BLACK BIRD

THE PRESENCE OF GOD

MODERN DAY POETRY

THE PRESENCE OF GOD

The presence of God is all the power that I need.

I have prepared myself mentally for the goods that I desire .I have the power over my conscience.

MODERN DAY POETRY

MY DECREE

I decree that my cycle of failure is over. I will be the one to cause my entire family to prosper.

I believe that I am ready for what I want and what I want is ready for me I am taking positive actions towards my goals. I am visualizing my success Success and more success. MaryAnn Freeman

SMILE

MODERN DAY POETRY

One morning I awoken and there was no smile to be found. I did not have any worries. But I could not smile. Until one day I saw a man. Who

Had no legs and no arms. He had a smile on his face. For some reasons. I could not understand. Why was he smiling? I said to myself. If The man has no legs and arms. He still has a smile on his face. From that day on. I learned to smile, I am bless. When my smile tries to leave me. I am seeing the vision of the man.

ROSES

Oh how I wish someone will buy me roses. I never held a rose in my hands before. I can smell the beautiful roses. Oh how I wish someone will buy me roses. There is a lady name Miss Rosie and every day she received roses. Oh how I wish someone will buy me roses. Miss Rosie always throw her roses away. She never enjoyed her roses. One day she is going to miss those roses. They are beautiful to smell and to hold. Oh how I wish someone will buy me roses.

ANGELS

I always believe in angels. I knew there was someone watching over me. I used to look up into the sky and talk to my angel. Surely my angels are with me. Where ever I go. You should ask yourself. Are your angels watching over you? What made me believe that my angels are watching over me. When I was crossing the street with my two children. A car came speeding. As me and my children was crossing. My angels was watching over us and save our life that day. Thank you my angels for watching over me and my children. Yes, I believe in angels

MODERN DAY POETRY

THIS IS A DIVINE SET UP

God has inspired me to write inspiring stories and poems. To put values back into the universe coming from a divine place. Where truth shines on a divine light and life. Over ourselves and the universe. I am bless to have this gift of a caring and loving compassion and giving spirit.

KNOCKING AT THE DOOR

If someone is knocking at your door .You cannot see him. You can feel him in your heart . Let him in. You will be glad that you did .He will make you feel new again. He will comfort you, and take away all your pains. Once you have opened .Your door and let him in. He will let you see. What you could not see before. If you will just open up the door . Some of us is bless. To hear him knocking at the door .Not everyone hears him knocking .When he is knocking at the door. Those who opens up their doors will see better days. Go ahead and open up the door. You will be glad that you opened up the door

HOME

Many of our children wants to leave home .They feel that they are not being treated right at home. So they decided to pack their bags and leave home without knowing .Where they are going. Why do you want to leave home? Did your mother are your father mistreat you? Did they hit you? I see your answer is no.. You want to leave home. Are you

MODERN DAY POETRY

saying that you are not being treated right at home? Then you have no other choice. You have to leave home. What do you think is going to happen to you? You do not know .If you will survive. At home you will still be alive and safe. I sai d to all children. If you do not have any problems at home stay home. For those children that have to leave home get good counseling.

THIS IS THE HOUSE THAT GOD BLESS

When I awaking in the morning and after praying. I stead in the middle of the floor and said out loud. This is the house that God has bless I heard a voice within said this house is bless. This house will not fall when the storm comes . This house stands on solid grounds and cannot be moved. There is a sign that hangs on my wall. The words said this is the house God has bless.

.

THE WINTER I NEVER CAN FORGET

How can I ever forget? It was a cold winter night. When my world came to an end. Every night I could hear my baby crying. This winter night . I could not hear my baby crying. I knew that something was wrong. I went into my baby's room. My baby was wrapped in the blanket .Oh my God . My baby turned pink and was cold as ice. All I could

.

MODERN DAY POETRY

do is hold my baby tight. During that winter cold night. It came and took my baby life. How can I ever forget that winter night? I will never forget that winter night that took my baby life.

TO MY SON JERMAINE BLINKY FREEMAN

My dear son. I did not see you. When you left and before dawn .You were gone. One minute you were here with us. The next minute you were gone. Your brothers and sisters and friends will miss you. I did not say good bye, and I felt very sad. Until you came to me in a dream .The dream seem so real. I remember the dream. When you came to me on February 17,1993, and I finally got to said goodbye to you my son Jermaine. I thought that you were dead. You came to me in a dream. We said goodbye. You looked at me with a smile on your face. We embrace each other. You came back to me in a dream .To let me know that you are at peace , When I awaking out of the dream. I was not feeling sad. My son you came to me in a dream. To tell me good bye, and you are resting in peace Jermaine . I am going to miss you. Your brothers and sisters and friends. We want you to rest in peace my son Jermaine. Me and your father is missing you. Now it is time for a mother to said goodbye my son Jermaine .Now that we have come to the end of the road. We will never forget you. Your spirit will always remained my son Jermaine.

SOLDIERS

Where are our soldiers? They went to war to fight. A battle that they knew nothing about. Many of them lost their life. Fighting a war that they knew nothing about . What about their families that they left behind? Because our soldiers went to fight a battle that they knew nothing about . I pray when our soldiers returned .They will get the honor and the rewards that they deserve. They families should not be in need are lacking anything. Our soldiers should never be homeless and jobless. After all they went to war to fight .A battle that they knew nothing about. So many

MODERN DAY POETRY

of our soldiers lost their life. Let us welcome our soldiers, and give them what they deserve. After all they fought for our country. Let our country take care of our soldiers

IF I HAD MY OWN LAW

If I had my own law. It will be a crime. To have people without food to eat and know where to sleep. If I had my own law. It will be a crime for children. Who disrespect their parents are adults. If I had my own law. People will not have to worry about their doctor bills. If I had my own law. There will be no more wars. If I had my own law. There will be peace and harmony in the world.

OFFICE R DAN

I am thinking. When I was a child. I used to play outside with my friends and cousins. We played all day. Until our parents called us to eat. Then we went back outside to play. We jumped rope and played hand ball and other games until dawn. We did not have to worry. Officer Dan watched our community. Everyone in the community knew officer Dan. Office Dan cared about our safety. We did not worry about anyone bothering us. Officer Dan was there to protect us. As I think back. I can see officer Dan. I wish the children of today had a officer Dan in their community. Who cares about the people and their community. Where there will be peace and harmony. We need more officers like office Dan.

CHILDREN

Children of today. Do not know how to play. I wish that I was a child. I would show the children of today how to play. Children of today. They sit around all day and play games. When I was a child. We played outside all day that gave us plenty of exercise. The children of today needs to learn how to play. How I wish that I was a child. I would show the children of today how to play. Time is going fast. I know things have changed. There is nothing wrong playing those video games. But children of today learn to play. Go outside and play and enjoy your child hood. While there is no problems facing you today. Oh how I wish that I was a child. I would go outside and play.

MODERN DAY POETRY

WHO SAID THAT A MAN IS NOT SUPPOSE TO CRY

Who said that a man is not suppose cry why? He goes through life struggles, and he is not suppose to cry. When he was a young boy. He was allowed to cry. Since he became a man. He is not allowed to cry. When he was a young boy. He suffers pain. So he had to cry. I said to any man. If you are suffering from deep pains. Go ahead and cry. It just means that you are human. It is not making you weaker. You are letting go that deep pain. Go ahead and cry. Who said that a man is not suppose to cry?

TOO LITTLE

I was angry this morning. I only had a little food to eat. I said to myself. How could this be? This should not happen to me. The little food that I had to eat. It seem as those it was too little. It did not seem as much. I was still angry. I turned on my TV, and seen the children with no food to eat. I was angry that I had too little food to eat. The children had no food to eat. Seeing the children without food to eat. I stop being angry about my food that I thought was too little. I am bless to have food to eat. Where the children had no food to eat. I said to myself. How can this be? We all should have food to eat. The next time that I think my food is too little. I will think about the children. Who had no food to eat. The children have to go to bed hungry every night. We must all help to feed our children and others. Who is without food to eat.

LOVE

Oh love are you a gift from God? Are we suppose to know how to love? Was love giving to us at birth? What happens If, you do not know how to love? Oh love do we have to learn to love? For so reason. I already knew how to love. Oh love was this a gift from above ? For us to love one another. I wish that everyone could lo. Then we can love each others.

MODERN DAY POETRY

MONEY

Money will no longer be a problem. When you learned to listen to God and keeping your faith and staying focus. God will reveal your calling. You may not recognize it the first time God will reveal it several times. You must pay attention to your dreams. Once God has revealed your calling. Then your passion will start to grow. Things will start to seem like a puzzle with all the pieces being put together by the universe. Money will be your least worry. Your passion and your calling will drawn money to you.

DARKNESS

Many days and many nights. I have seen men of darkness roam about There is no rest for them. Even when the light begins to shine. They still remained in darkness Sometimes. I wonder why. There is so much darkness in the world. Then a thought came across my mind. If it was no darkness in the world .Many things would not be Men of darkness was born into darkness. They knew In order to succeed . They had to work harder To overcome their darkness Even thought they knew that they will always be a shadow over them.Men of darkness is not letting that stop them. They knew that they have to work harder. They labor tells the stories .It tells theirs history of their creation and out of their darkness came light.

MY KNIGHT

I t was night, and you were dress in black. I knew you had to fight this night my knight. Sometime during the night.You made your flight. I pray that you do not loss your life tonight. I could see your armor shining as bright as light. Oh how I am going to miss you my knight. I knew you had to fight to night my knight . I hope and pray that you come back to me safe my knight.

MAKING A DECISION

MODERN DAY POETRY

Sometimes we all have to make a decision that we do not want to make. We hope that when we do make a decision it is the right one. When I have to make a decision. I wait and listen for God to guild me .No one really wants to make a decision that concerning a love one. It is hard to make a decision . When it is your love ones it hurts the most .You want to make the right decision. I hope and pray. When you have to make a decision for your love ones. It is the right decision .I listen to God to guild me.It leaves me with a clear conscience.

ROOM 1904

It was nice to get away. I enjoyed room 1904. When I first walked into room 1904.I felt a peace that came over me. The time that I spend in room 1904 .My mind was at peace. I was able to hear myself think clearly . I could feel the peace in my spirit in room 1904. Before I left. I stood by the door and said goodbye room 1904.You gave me so much comfort and peace

DOCTOR

Doctor can you help my brother? He is very sick. No doctor my brother do not have insurance. Doctor can you please help my brother ? Oh I see you cannot help my brother. Because he has no insurance. Doctor who can I call? My brother is very sick, and he needs a doctor. Doctor can you please help my brother? So your turning my brother away. Because he has no insurance. Sadly to said my brother died last night. Because doctor you turned my brother away. My brother had no insurance, Maybe the next patient. You will help. It should not matter about the insurance only the patient life

MY UNIVERSE

When I close my eyes. I can see the bright lights. My body feels light as though I am flowing. My spirit is being lifted and flowing freely. The moon is so bright. The air is fresh and my energy is high. In my mind. I am flowing through time. The clouds surround me.They are white as snow. I can enjoy my universe by closing my eyes

LONG ISLAND

MODERN DAY POETRY

Albertha lived in the city. She always dreamed of visiting her grandmother in Long Island. She wanted to play in her grandmother's big yard. Albertha could not wait to go to her grandmother's house in Long Island .She knew that the experience would be different than the city. Albertha was so excited . When she arrived at her grandmother's house .She seen the beautiful houses and the big yards. It did not take long for Albertha . To experience playing with the children in Long Island. She met a girl name Myra. Myra showed her. Her Mickey Mouse collections . Albertha was starting to feel sad. She knew that she will be leaving soon . She will miss her new friend Myra. Albertha lived in the city all her life . When she arrived to her grandmother's house. It seen as thought it was a different world . When Albertha returned to the city. She told all her friends about the beautiful houses and the big yards in Long Island . Albertha told her friends that they should visit Long Island. They will experience a different world

MODERN DAY POETRY

One might say why? Do she calls her poems Modern Day Poetry. Her poems does not rhyme. My poems are a form of expressions and does not have to rhyme It expresses my thoughts of today realty. My conscience is in tune with to day's realty. So I write from the view of my expressions. My poetry expresses my conscience view of today's events,

COUNTRY GIRL

I want me a country girl. You see these city girls are too fast for me .The country girls knows how to cook and sew. A city girl will tell me. I need to learn. How to cook and sew. A country girl will love you with all her heart. She wears her regular blue jeans. Where a city girl wants to wear design jeans. I want me a country girl. She knows how to care for me. A city girl may not care. I want me a country girl. She will appreciate me. A city girl will say. This is what you suppose to do. I want me a country girl.

MOTHERS

MODERN DAY POETRY

Where are the babies ? They told me that babies are born and being left behind. Mothers are having babies and leaving them behind. This is sad that babies are being born and left behind. Did anyone see the mothers of these babies? We all need to give a helping hand. Too many babies are being left behind. Some are found alive and some have already died. There are some babies. We will never found. Where are the babies mothers? We all have to give a helping hand. Let the mothers know that there is help. Too many babies are being left behind. Mothers do not be afraid to reach out for help. No more leaving babies behind.

BELIEVE

Stop all of your crying and dry your eyes. All you have to do is believe with all your heart. Do the right thing and do not doubt. Your dreams will come true. Hold on to your vision and your dreams and believe.

MODERN DAY POETRY

MODERN DAY POETRY

Ii is sad to be sad. When you do not have to be .It is sad to Cry. When you are not suppose to cry .Because people will not leave you alone.They do not want to see a smile on your face They want you to be sad. Because you want to put a smile on someone else face. It is sad to be sad when you do not have to be sad. It is sad to cry .When you do not have to cry .They will not leave us alone. They do not want us to put a smile on some else face.

PEOPLE NEED TO LAUGH AGAIN

People need to laugh together again. When was the last time you seen people laughing together. People don't laugh together anymore. In our great big world .It so much hate and confusing. We should all learn to love one another .It does matter. Where you come from .When was the last time you seen people laughing together? We all need to learn from one another. So we can come together and love one another. Why is there so much confusing and disbelief in this great big world that we live In this world there is plenty of room for all of us. We should not have to fight one another .Why should there be separate this and separate that. Let us learn to laugh together again just like the children .When they are playing. They learned to play and laugh together .This big world that we live in would be a better place for all mankind So let us laugh together again.

I HAD TO DIG DOWN DEEP

MODERN DAY POETRY

I had dig down deep and bring out what needs to be, So the world can see .I am I am somebody. There was a time in my life. I Thought that I was nobody. But I had to dig down deep and bring out what need to be. So the world can see I am somebody .I thought that I had to become somebody .Until the lord came and set me on the throne and guild me. When the lord came in . I had to dig down deep and brought out what needed to be .So the world can see. Now I am Somebody. Now the whole world is looking at me. I had to dig deep to bring out what suppose to be and for the world to see.

I LEARNED TO LOVE THYSELF

I use to look in the mirror and did not like what I saw .I would walk by the mirror. Until a little voice whisper to me and said stop .Look into the mirror .What do you see ?The voice told me to repeat these words out loud. I am loving and loveable, Compassion, kindness, Worthy Dependable strength of character and intellect, faith and power.The little voice whisper repeat these words over and over. Until you believe that you are worthy and love thyself

GIVING THANKS TO GOD

Before I close my eyes at night I thank god for giving me peace at night, and before I raise I praise him for letting me see another day. I could spend all my life giving thanks to god. He has been so wonderful to me and my family. He has been loving, caring and have giving me so much hope, and joy and most of all love that stays within my heart. Yes I could spend the rest of my life giving thanks to god. God has made me .Who I am today.

MODERN DAY POETRY

Without him there will be no me and n where to go. Now I have hope and no which way to go. I give my thanks to God. If I said thanks a million time. It still will not be enough. I could never give enough thanks to God. Until my last days and that is when my life has passed .Before I go with my last breath .I will give thanks to god on my dying bed.

WRITER

As a inspire writer. My writing flow with ease. It as though a higher power is guiding me .I am able to finish my writing without stopping .Until the writing is completed I Know that my inspiration comes from a higher power .Being able to write with such freedom and joy. This is why I know my gifts for writing comes from above. My calling is to write.

COLOR

So many of us comes in different color. What ever color we are .It should not matter. Because we are all from the same creator, and should my shade of color or your color make a difference .Because one shade of color is lighter than the other. I hope not. Because we are all from same creator .If I should have the knowledge and became successful in what I am doing. Should the doors close in my face .Just to let someone else take my place. Because of my color. . When we are all from the same creator .Each and every one of us have no control over our color. But we do have a choice in the way .We want to choose to live our life. We want to have the choose the goals in life. If success is what we are aiming for, and we have the knowledge and met the challenge .Then the doors should not close in our face. Just for someone else to take our place. Because of our color .we

MODERN DAY POETRY

are all from the same creator and to him it does not matter. What our colors are .So unlock the doors. So that we of colors can enjoy our success just like the others.

PAIN

As I stare into your eyes I can see nothing but pain in your eyes my darling .Why are you suffering ? She is not the one you love and that the reason .There so much pain in your eyes yes, you try to hide the pain. It will not go away. Oh my love. I knew that she was not the one you love. It was once said that a man's heart bears the pain.But darling as I stare into your eyes. I can see the pain in your eyes .instead of your heart .Darling you cannot hide your eyes and that how I can tell that something is wrong, Because darling it shows .She is not the one you love. You do not want to hurt her. So you are bearing so much pain .Because she is not the one you love. Your are in so much pain. Darling I can tell by your eyes that there is pain. Tell her the truth to ease your pain.

PAID MY DUES

They said that she thinks. She is this said she is that.Well I have to stand and said. When my children did not have any food to eat .and there was only slices of bread to eat. I divided that bread for all to eat. When my laundry needed to be wash I scrub them clean on my hands. When my toilet was dirty . I got down on my knees and scrub .Until it was clean

MODERN DAY POETRY

. Yes, I paid my dues .When my man comes home from work feeling stress. I let my man lean on me. Until he go strong . They said that she thinks. She is this and she is that. Well I never ran from a situation. I stead strong .Worked odd jobs. Came home and took care of my children. Giving my very best. Not once did I beg. I made no excuses. Because I knew that I had to keep going on. I thank God for the strength. Yes, I am this and I am that

VICTORY

You laugh to keep from crying and to keep going on. Because you know once you give up. You are the real loser. So you keep going on no matter what. Some time you have to laugh out laugh to keep from crying. You cannot give up. You came to far. You know that there will be better days. You be laughing. It will not be to keep from crying It will be because you made it through. Not once this you give up. You bears all the ups and downs and stood strong. Through it . You came out with a smile of victory on your face.

OPPORTUNITY

All my life I have been search for opportunities and through my searching. I became depress and impatient with anxiety. Left me with a lot of stress. Because I had search so long and could not found success. I was looking at so many opportunities. None of them meet my needs. Until one day. I decided to look within myself. Not realizing that opportunity was there all the time within me. I did not know this. Until I accepted Jesus into my life. Where opportunity was giving to me through the grace of Jesus Christ. I found out that opportunity was waiting on me all the time.

LIVING IN A WORLD OF MY OWN

I want to live in a world of my own. So what if people said that I am strange. I want to live in a world of my own. If, I live in your world. Would you promise peace, love,happiness and togetherness and justice for all are turn

MODERN DAY POETRY

your heads. If you can promise this. Then I will live in your world.If not I want to live in a world of my own. Because I can control my own world. Can you control your world? Then bring back peace, love and happiness and most of all justice for all. Until you do. I want to live in a world of my own.

DRUGS

I feel sadness in my heart to see. So many people losing their life to drugs. . For another man's gain. Why are we helping to destroy another human life. When we should be trying to support them. Not trying to gain on others weakness. What is happening to our world today? Does anyone cares? How we as people is treating and caring for each others. Should we influence our people to do drugs. I feel the sadness in my heart. Because it not right. This is being done without any conscience involve. Destroying others life. Until it happen to someone that they love. Then reality set in that is was not right. Now your love is gone for doing drugs. I hope your conscience is telling you to stop selling those drugs and bring back hope instead of dope..

THE CHILD THAT LIVES WITHIN MY WOMB

Mother I can feel your hurt and your crying. But I could not help you. I was living inside your womb. Mother I did not mean for you to suffering so much carrying me in your womb. When you hurt I hurt and when you cry I cry. The difference is your crying on the outside. I am crying on the inside. I did not mean to hurt you so much mother. I wish there was away that there was no pains for you to bear. Because I also bear those pains. Mother I can feel your hurt and pain and crying. Sometime I wonder. If you wanting me. Mother I did not mean to hurt you. I could not help. Because I was in your womb. Mother we both made it through.

AWAKING

MODERN DAY POETRY

Through out my life. There has been many struggles and pain. Even being treated unjustly. I could not understand why. There was so much pain in my life. It seem as though the answer will never come. Going through so much pain and struggles . Have made me .Who I am today. Gong through this struggles and pain. Has brought me to a higher level of understanding my true self. I am no longer asleep. I have awaking to my divine conscience self. My calling is to inspire others through my writing.

NO BODY LOVES ME

Little Mary's grandmother would sit in her rocking chair every day. All she would said no body loves me in all my life. I have felt alone. Little Mary could not understand. Why her grand mother keep said that nobody loves me. It made little Mary start thinking to herself. Grandmother do not know about Jesus. Little Mary was afraid to ask her grand mother. Because she thought is was a foolish question. Because her grand mother was much older and of cause she knew about Jesus. As the days passed by. Her grandmother was still said that nobody loves me. Once again it made little Mary start thinking to herself. Grandmother knows nothing about Jesus. Now this time little Mary was confuse. She still did not understand. Why her grandmother did not know Jesus. Being confuse she left her grand mother's room. She waiting until her grandmother went to sleep. Then she went back into her grandmother's mother room. She placed a bible by her grandmother side and she left the room. When her grandmother awaking. She felt a bible my her side . Little Mary grand mother pick up the bible and start to read. As she was reading the bible. The tears started running down her face. Finally before little Mary grand mother died. She realize that she was loved all the time.

THE BLUE SKY

I keep having a vision and my vision only shows the blue sky, and I did not know why. I keep seeing the blue sky.The blue in the sky seems so bright and clear.My vision is so clear as though I can reach out and touch the sky. I close my eyes. But the vision would not leave me. So I said to myself tonight, When I go to sleep the

MODERN DAY POETRY

vision will leave me by morning. It so strange. When I awaking in the morning the vision was already there. Before I open my eyes,and all I could see was the blue sky. I just keep asking myself why am I having the vision .I even try closing my eyes while I was sitting up in my chair, but the vision was still there, and all I could see was the blue sky .Finally it was night again ,and I said to myse. Maybe when I close my eyes this time and awake in the morning.The vision will be gone. Yes my vision did leave during the night, but before the vision left. The vision took me closer to the blue sky as though I was in the sky .The vision showed the beautiful sky ,and how the blue stood out in the sky I cannot explain it all. When I awaking in the morning. The first thing I did .I looked up at the blue sky.

MODERN DAY POETRY
BY MARYANN FREEMAN
POEMS

SMILE, ,ROSES,ANGELS,THIS IS A DIVINE SET UP,KNOCKING AT YOUR KNOCK,HOME,THIS IS THE HOUSE THAT GOD BLESS,THE WINTER I NEVER FORGET,DEDICATED TO MY SON JERMAINE, SOLDIERS, IF I HAD MY OWN LAW,OFFICE DAN,CHILDREN,WHO SAID THAT A MAN IS NOT SUPPOSE TO CRY,TOO LITTLE,LOVE,MONEY, DARKNESS, KNIGHT, MAKING A DECISION. ROOM 1904, ,DOCTOR,UNIVERSE,LONG ISLAND, MODERN DAY POETRY,COUNTRY GIRL, MOTHER, BELIEVE, PEOPLE NEED TO LAUGH,I HAD TO DIG DEEP , I LEARNED TO LOVE THY SELF,GIVING THANKS TO GOD ,WRITER,COLOR,PAIN,PAID MY DUE S,VICTORY. OPPORTUNITY,LIVING IN A WORLD OF MY OWN.DRUGS, THE CHILD THAT LIVES IN MY WOMB,AWAKING,NO BODY LOVES ME,BLUE SKY,MODERN DAY POETRY,REACHING THE TOP,INSPIRE WRITER,OLD BILLY,BLACK BIRD

MODERN DAY POETRY

This book is dedicated to my beloved husband and son. Daniel Freeman Senior, and Jermaine Freeman. Also my beloved mother Albertha E Fields. I want to thank my loving sons Daniel Freeman Jr and Jarrel Freeman for their continue love and support.

I hope my poems will be Inspiring to all.

I want to thank Oprah and Deepak . For their 21day's of meditation getting unstuck. I also wants to thank Shanel Cooper Sykes. For recommended the book.Think and Grow Rich

MODERN DAY POETRY

REACHING THE TOP

So you have finally made it. You want through strugglers and pain. You never gave up It was worth all the sweat and tears. Now that you have reach the top. I only ask one thing of you. Reach down your hands to help lift another up. So that persons can reach down their hands to lift up another. Keep reaching down to help lift others. So that we can lift as many as we can leave no one behind.

INSPIRE WRITER

I am a inspire writer. When I start to write it flow easy. Until my work is completed. When I am writing. Ido not get stuck. Because the idea is already completed in my mind. There is a force. When I am writing that makes my writing flow easy. My writing is a gift that is coming from a divine place. I am an inspire writer.When I am inspire. I do not have to worry.

MODERN DAY POETRY

Old Billy was a good old soul. He got along with everyone in town. Billy goes to his favor bar. Oh Billy was known for spending his money .Buying drinks for everyone. He did not mind spending his money. One day Billy won the lottery. The news got out all over town that Old Billy won the lottery .A beautiful young lady walked into the bar. Everyone in town was telling Billy. You better watch. How you are spending your money. Oh Billy yelled out loud and laugh .He said there is plenty more. Where that comes from. Billy and the young lady got marry. Still everyone in town was telling Billy. You better watch . How you are spending your money. Oh Billy laugh out loud again. He yelled there is plenty. Where that comes from. His wife was buying fancy clothes. Everyone in town knew that soon old Billy will be broke.One evening Billy walked into the bar looking sad. His wife was gone and all of his lottery money was gone. Someone yelled out. I hope you watch over your money. Old Billy did not laugh out this time. His wife and money was gone. Billy said my wife and all my money is gone.Old Billy laugh out loud and said .I was a fool. But I was a happy old fool.

BLACK BIRD

Did you ever see a black bird fly in the sky? He flies so high in the sky As though he is touching the clouds. I like seeing the black bird flying in the sky. He flies so high in the sky. As thought he was a eagle that flies so high in the sky. Every night. When I close my eyes. I can see that black bird fly so high in the sky. Did you even see a black bird fly? He looks so beautiful. Flying high in the blue sky. I miss the black bird. Flying so high in the sky .When I open my eyes in the morning. The black bird is not there, Until tonight my black bird .When me eyes are close tight

MODERN DAY POETRY

www.ingramcontent.com/pod-product-compliance
Lightning Source LLC
Chambersburg PA
CBHW070921180426
43192CB00038B/2153